10 for $10 SHEET MUSIC
Classical Favorites

CONTENTS

TITLE	COMPOSER	PAGE
JESU, JOY OF MAN'S DESIRING	JOHANN SEBASTIAN BACH	2
MOONLIGHT SONATA (1ST MOVEMENT)	LUDWIG VAN BEETHOVEN	6
WALTZ IN A MINOR	FRÉDÉRIC CHOPIN	11
CLAIR DE LUNE	CLAUDE DEBUSSY	14
RHAPSODY IN BLUE (THEME)	GEORGE GERSHWIN®	20
THE MASTERPIECE (RONDEAU)	JEAN-JOSEPH MOURET	42
RONDO ALLA TURCA	WOLFGANG AMADEUS MOZART	28
THEME FROM PIANO CONCERTO No. 21 *(ELVIRA MADIGAN)*	WOLFGANG AMADEUS MOZART	34
RHAPSODIE ON A THEME OF PAGANINI	SERGEI RACHMANINOFF	38
FLIGHT OF THE BUMBLE BEE	NIKOLAI RIMSKY-KORSAKOV	45

Alfred Publishing Co., Inc.
16320 Roscoe Blvd., Suite 100
P.O. Box 10003
Van Nuys, CA 91410-0003
alfred.com

Copyright © MMVIII by Alfred Publishing Co., Inc.
All rights reserved. Printed in USA.

ISBN-10: 0-7390-5642-5
ISBN-13: 978-0-7390-5642-4

Cover photograph: Interior of empty theater, piano at center stage, elevated view © matton.com/Ivan Hunter

JESU, JOY OF MAN'S DESIRING

By J.S. BACH

MOONLIGHT SONATA

By LUDWIG VAN BEETHOVEN

Adagio sostenuto
Very delicately, with pedal throughout.

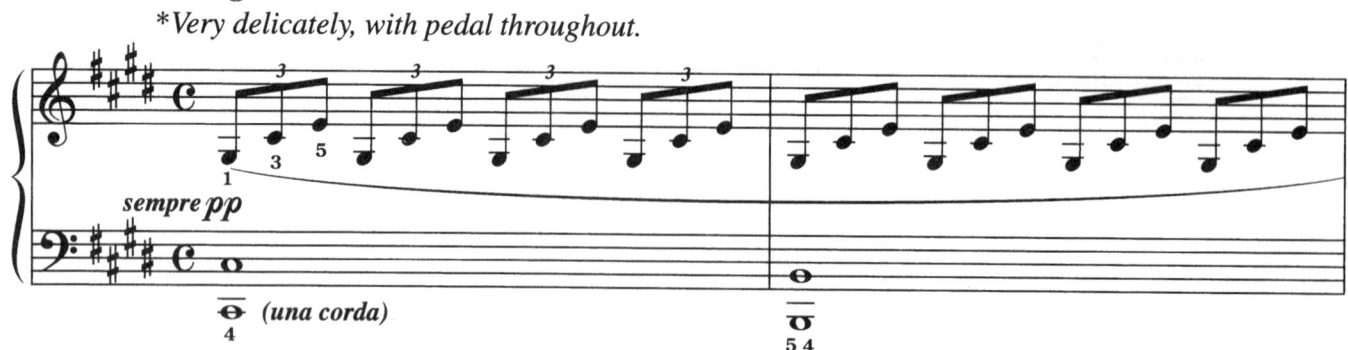

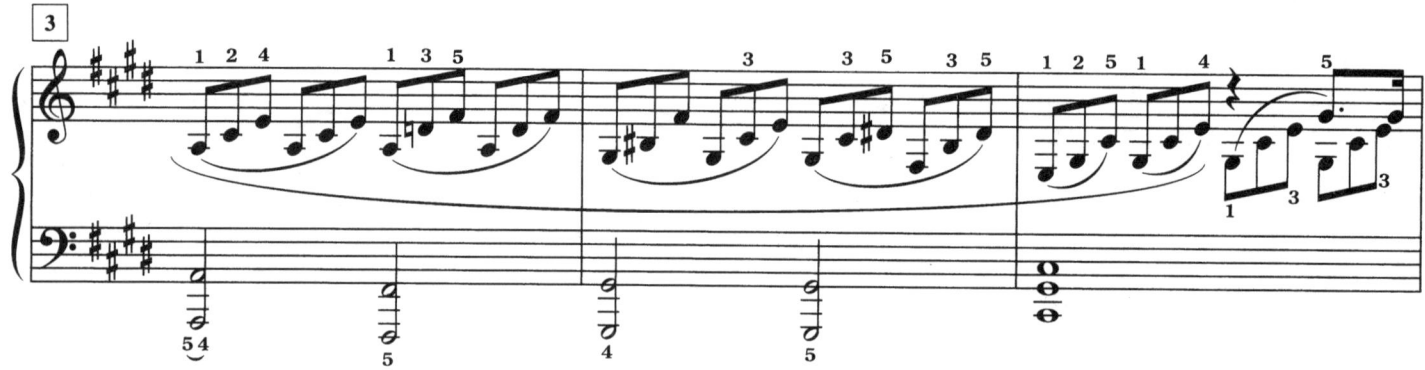

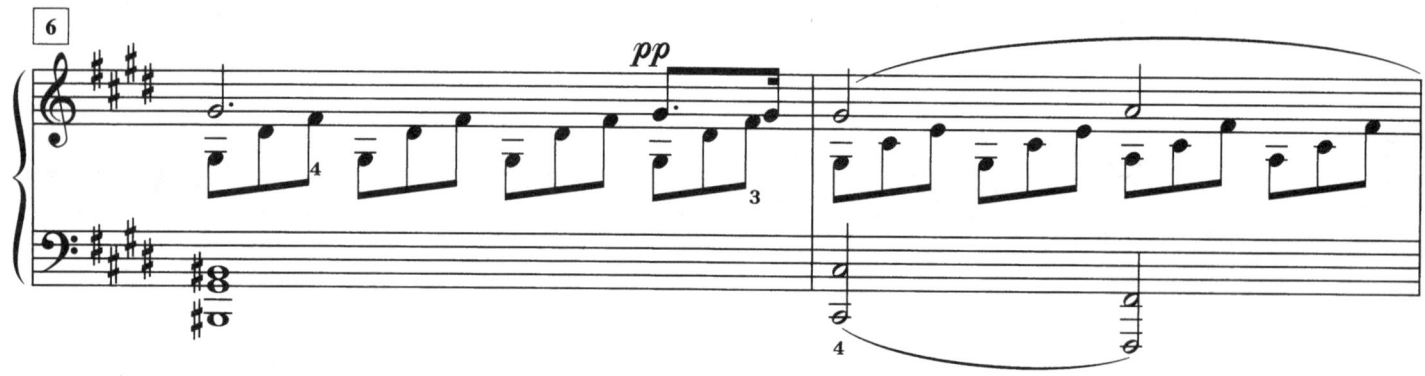

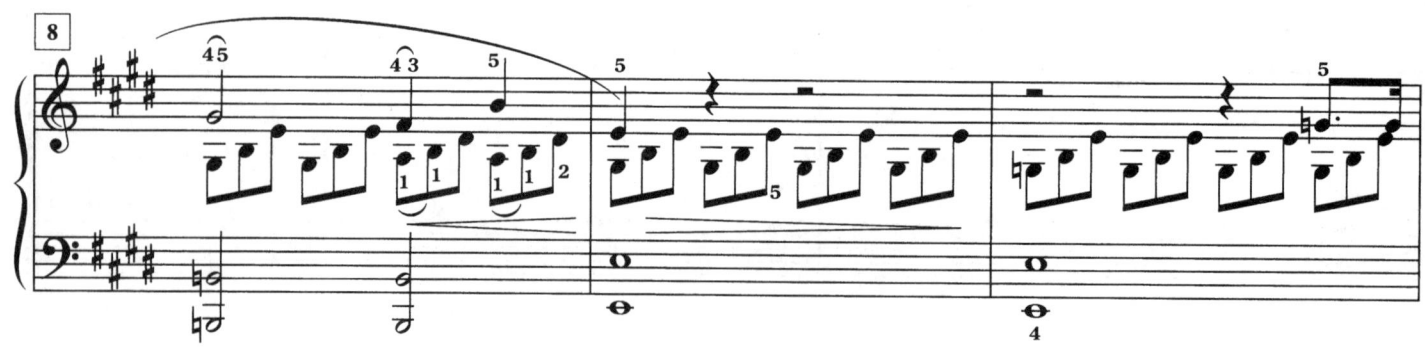

Moonlight Sonata - 5 - 1

© 2008 ALFRED PUBLISHING CO., INC.
All Rights Reserved

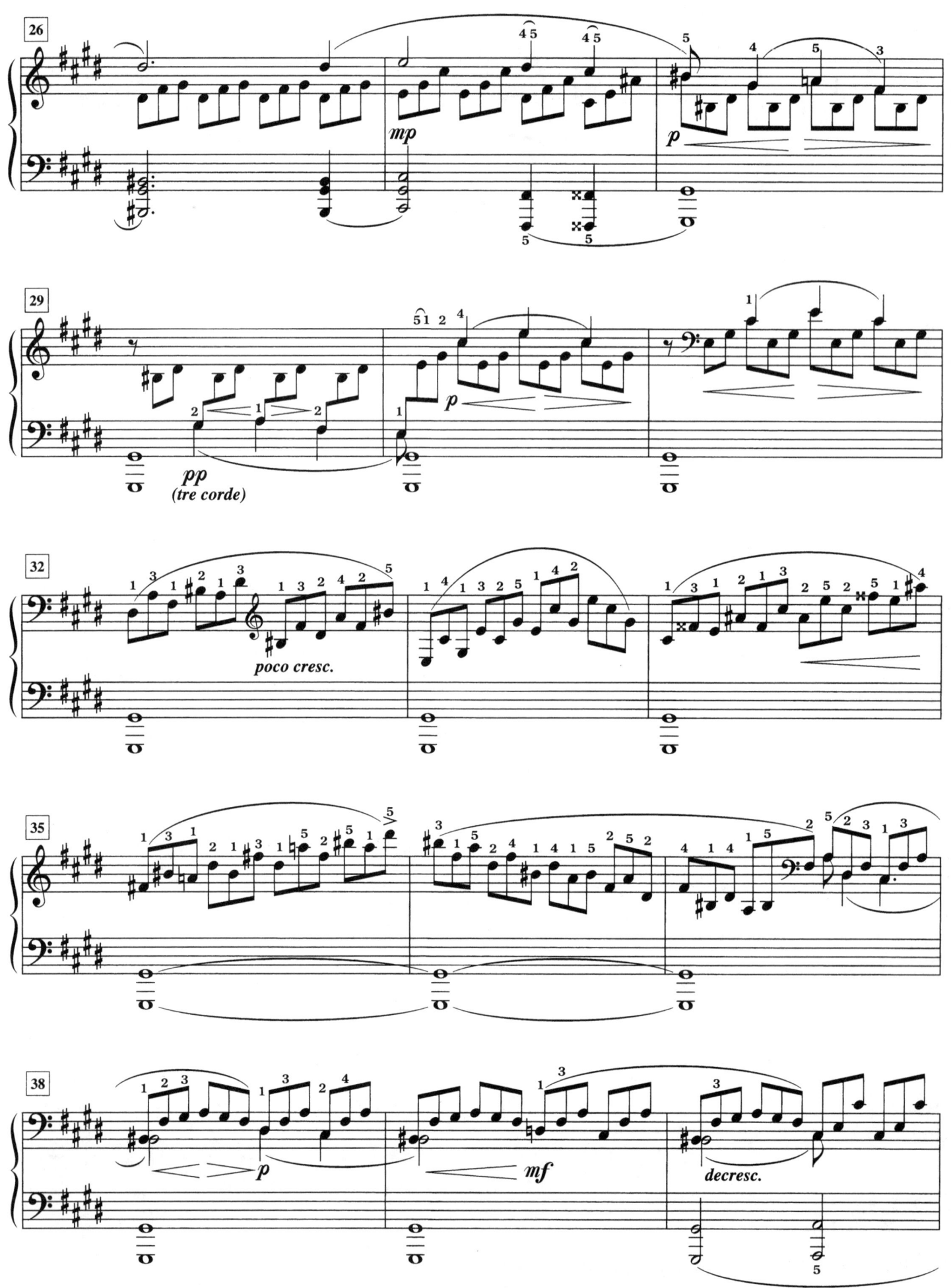

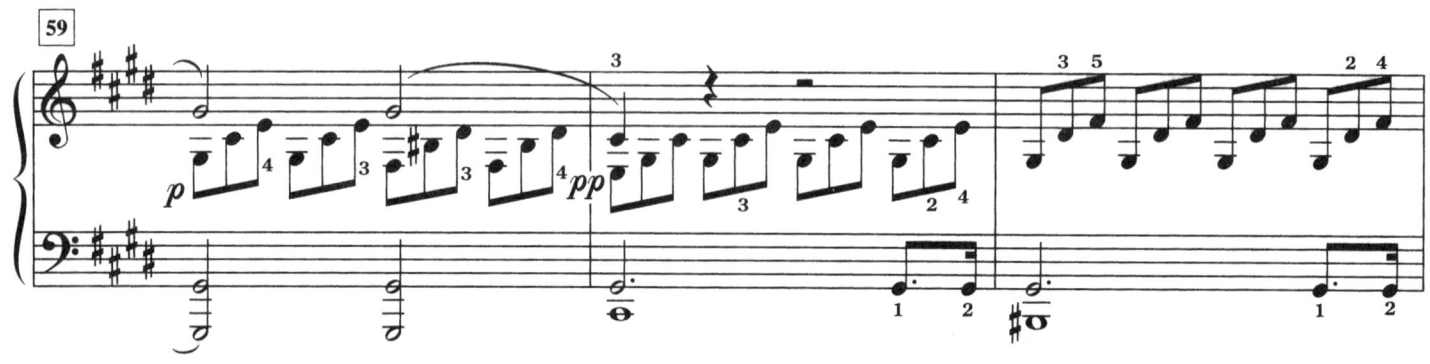

WALTZ IN A MINOR

By FREDERIC CHOPIN

Waltz in A Minor - 3 - 1

© 2008 ALFRED PUBLISHING CO., INC.
All Rights Reserved

CLAIR DE LUNE

By CLAUDE DEBUSSY

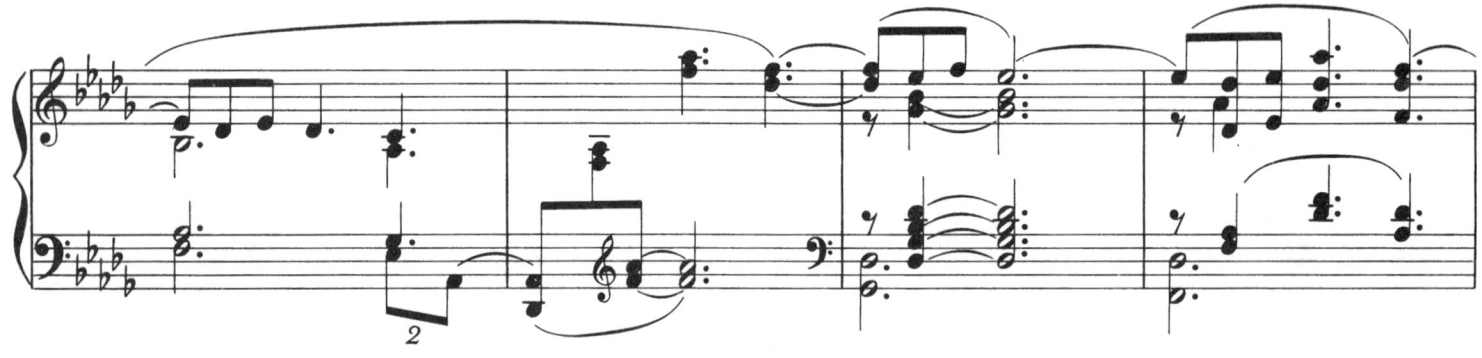

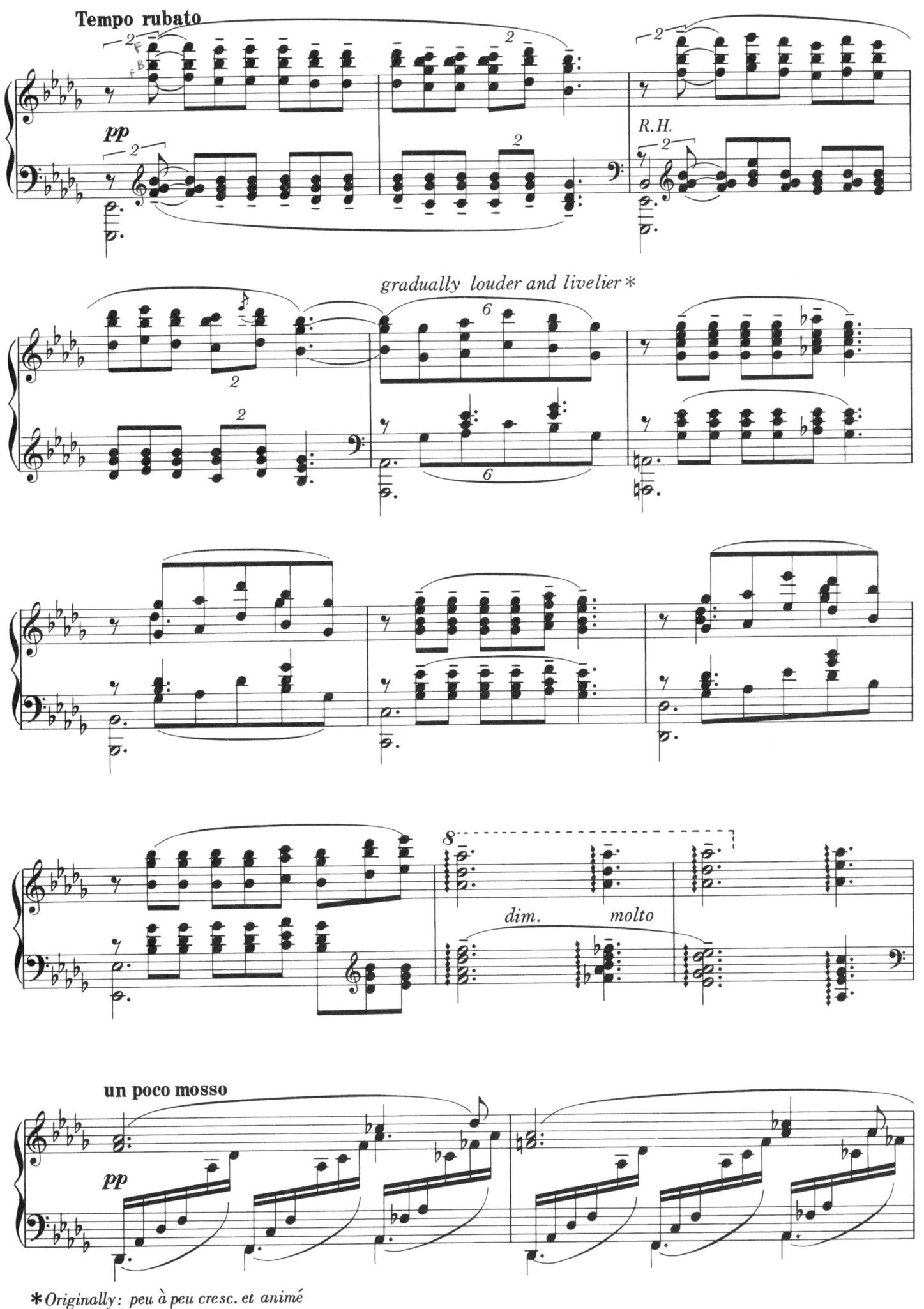

*Originally: peu à peu cresc. et animé

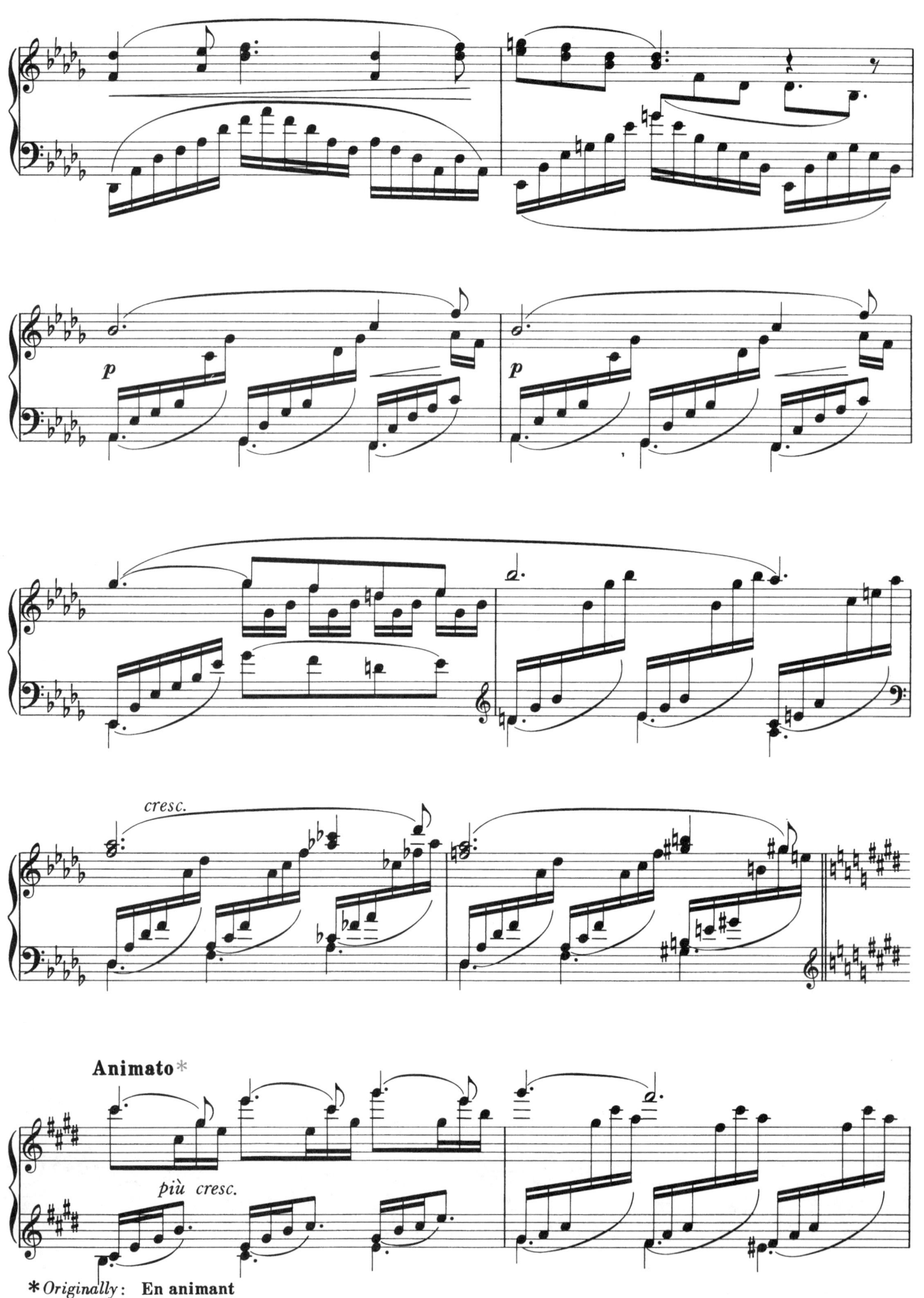

*Originally: **En animant**

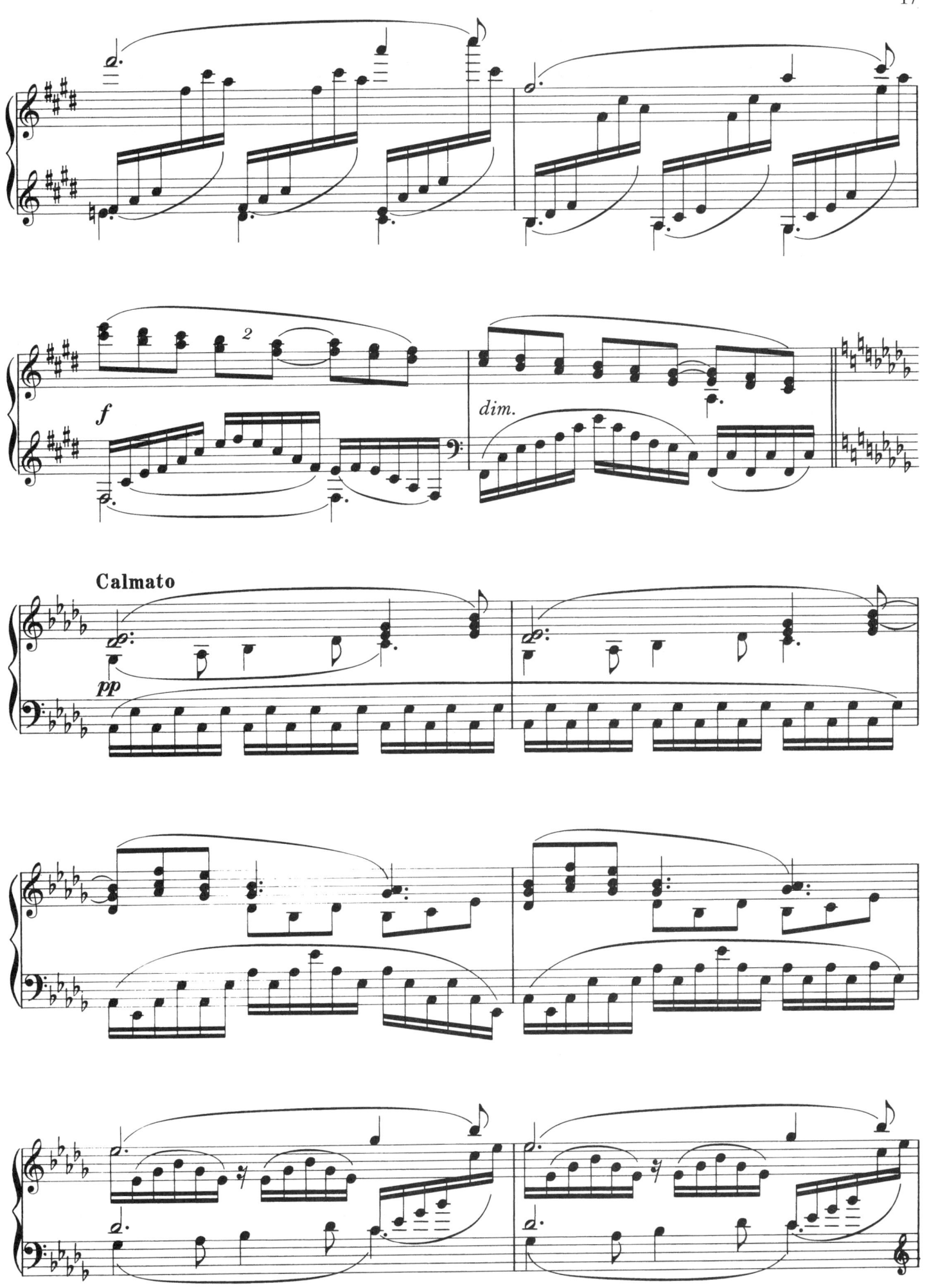

*Originally: morendo jusqu'à la fin

RHAPSODY IN BLUE

By GEORGE GERSHWIN

© 1924 (Renewed) WB MUSIC CORP.
GERSHWIN® and GEORGE GERSHWIN® are Registered Trademarks of Gershwin Enterprises
RHAPSODY IN BLUE™ is a Trademark of the George Gershwin Family Trust
All Rights Reserved

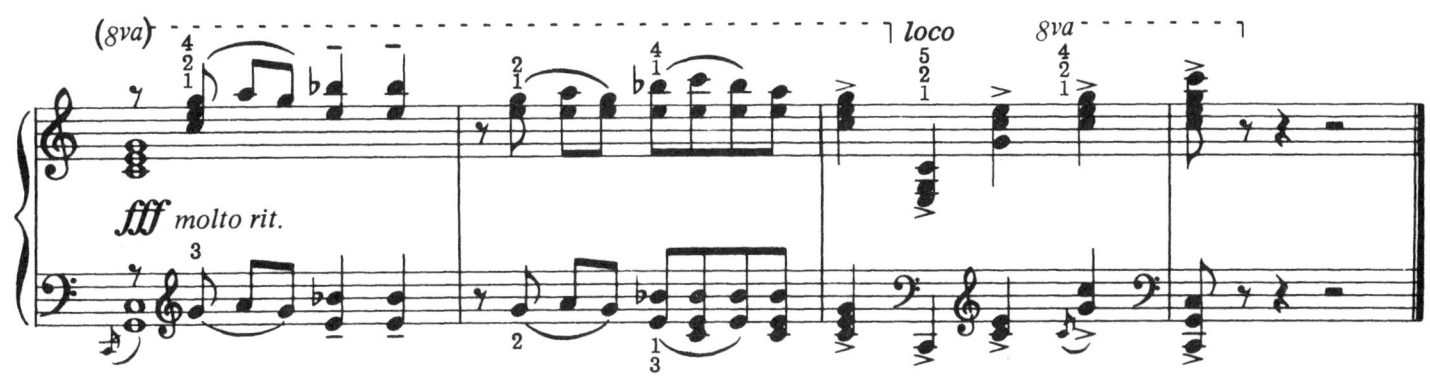

RONDO ALA TURCA

By W.A. MOZART

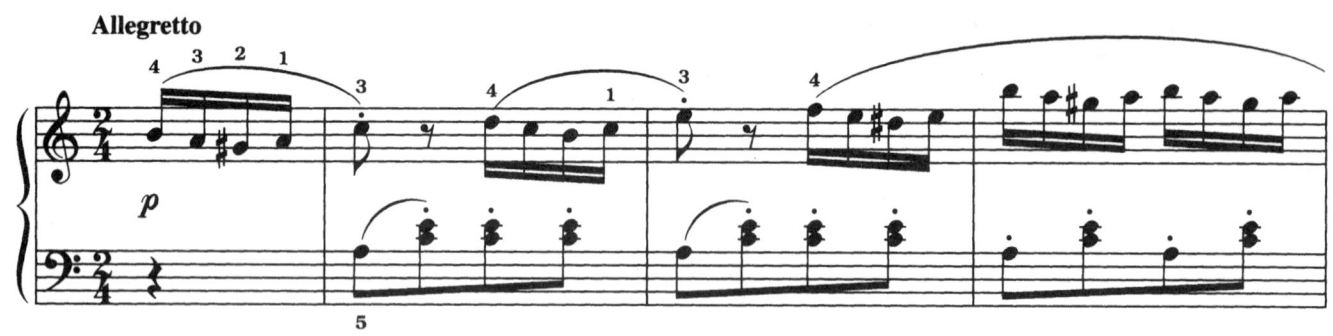
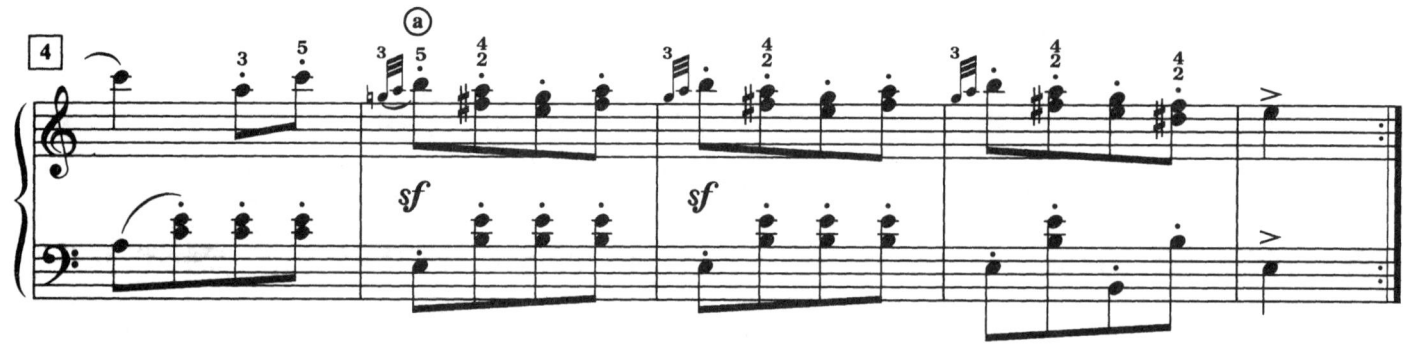
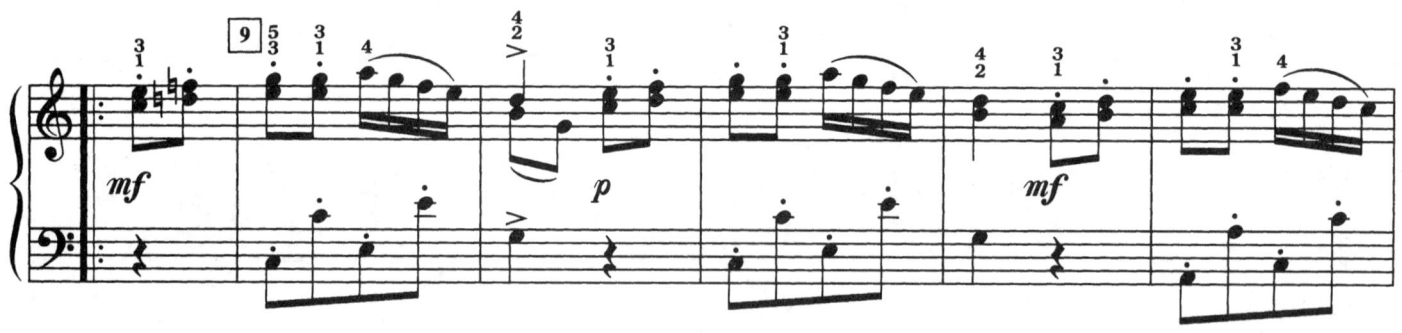

(b) Play the three small notes *very quickly*, with the first one *on the beat*.

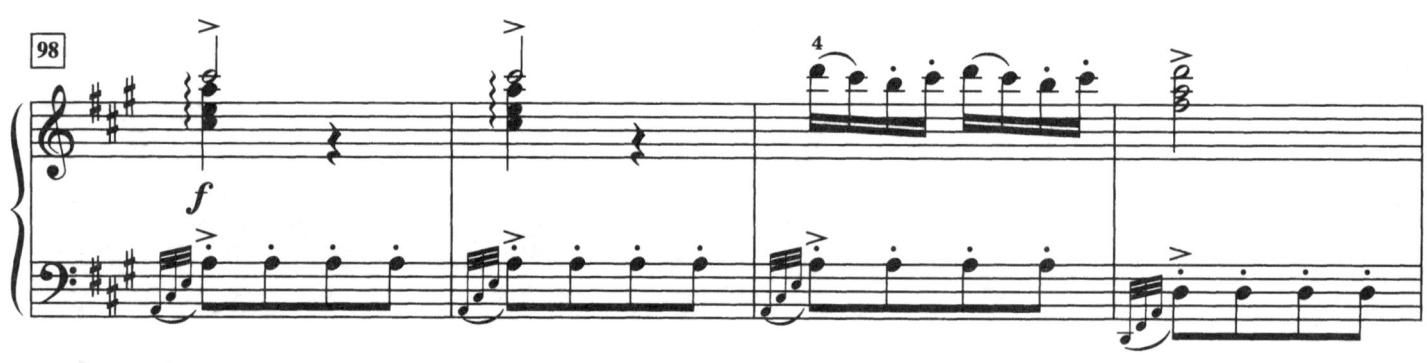

(a) Begin the trill on the upper note (F).

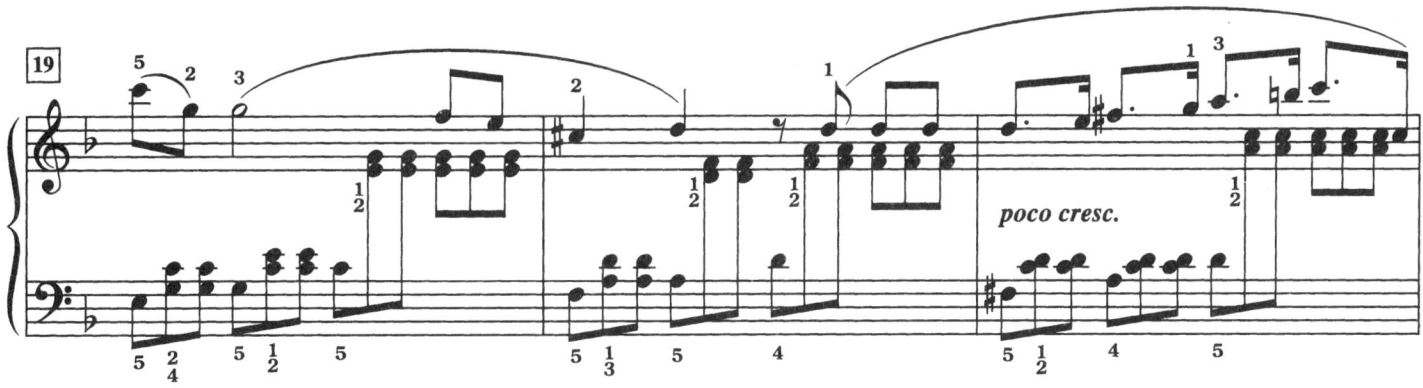
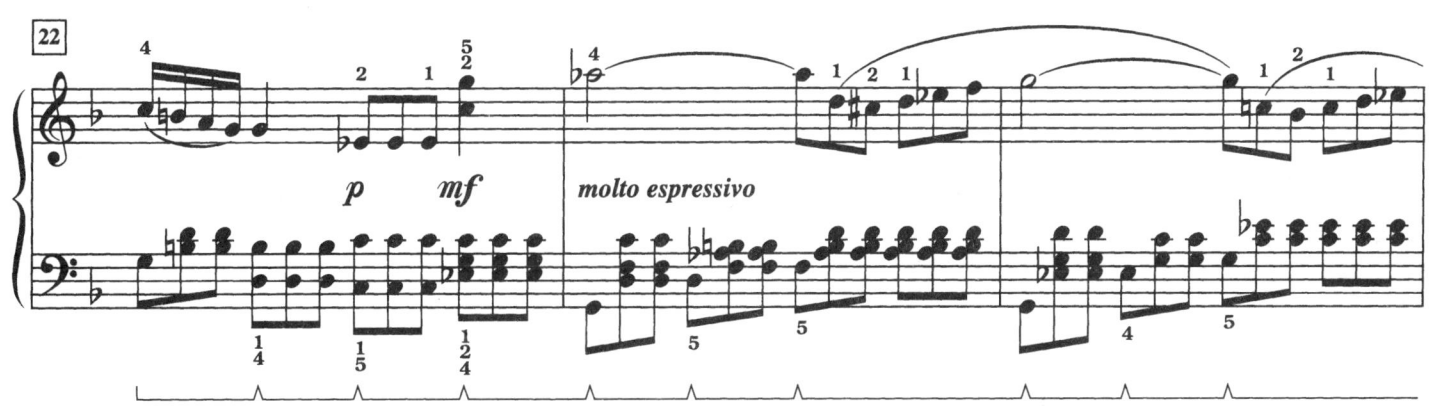

Theme from Concerto #21 - 4 - 2

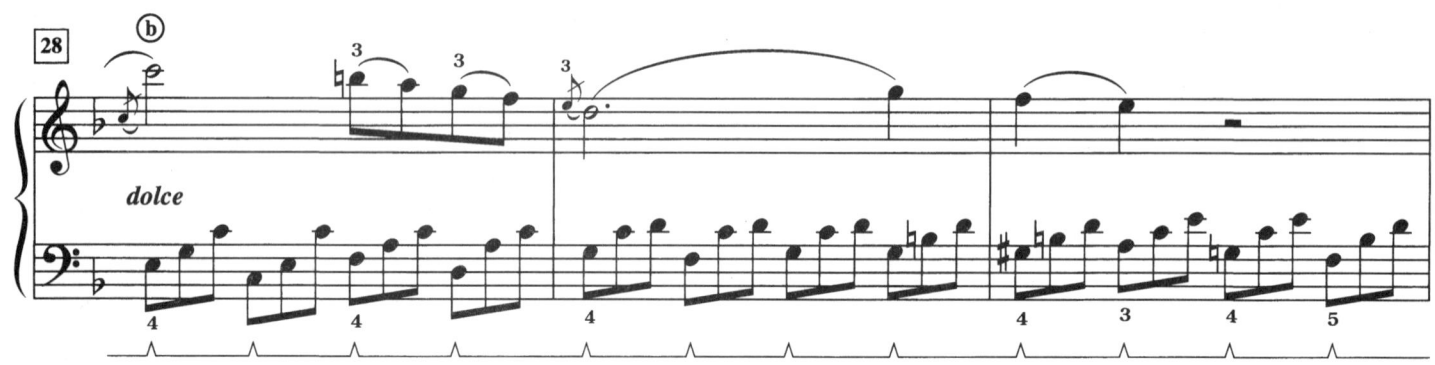
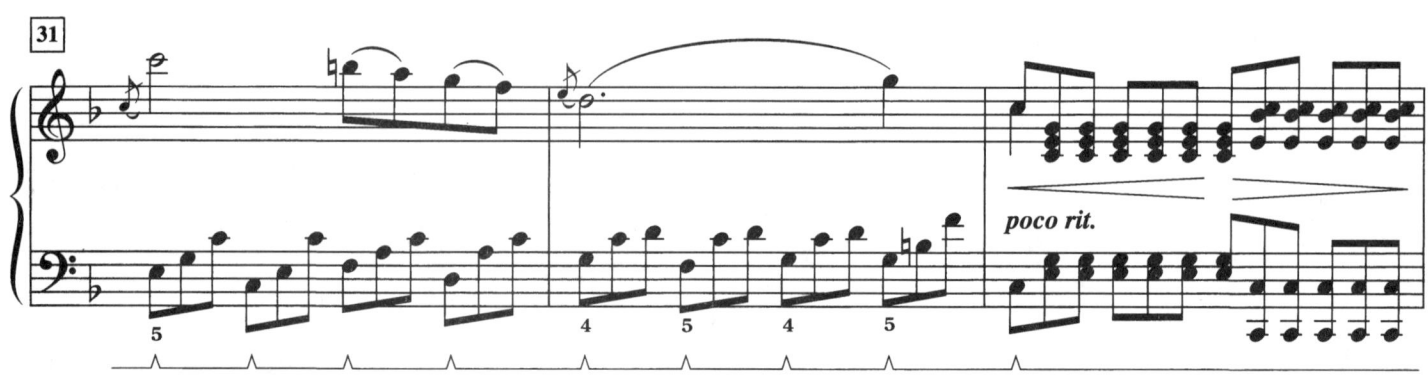

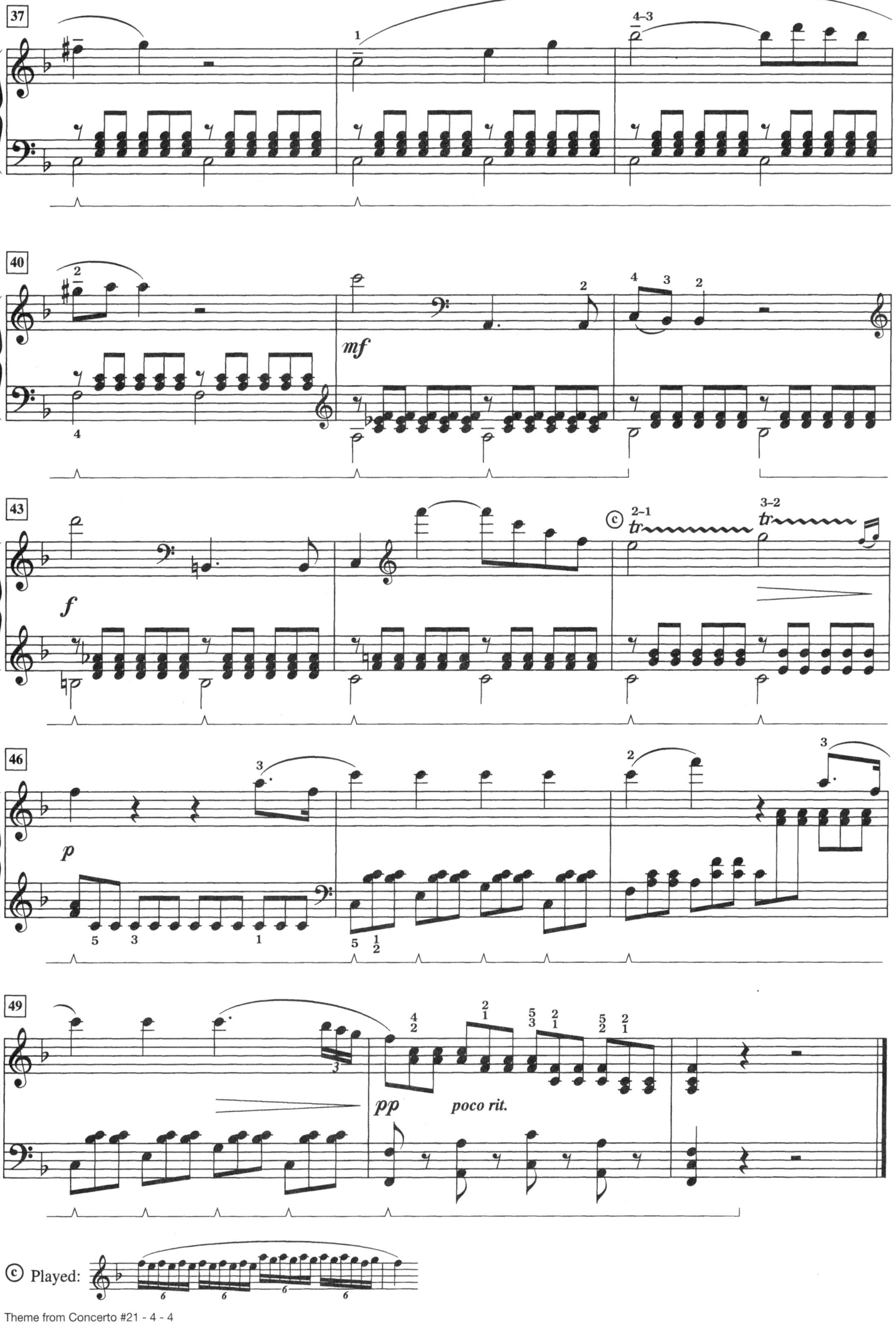
37
40
mf
43
f
tr
tr
46
p
49
pp
poco rit.
Played:

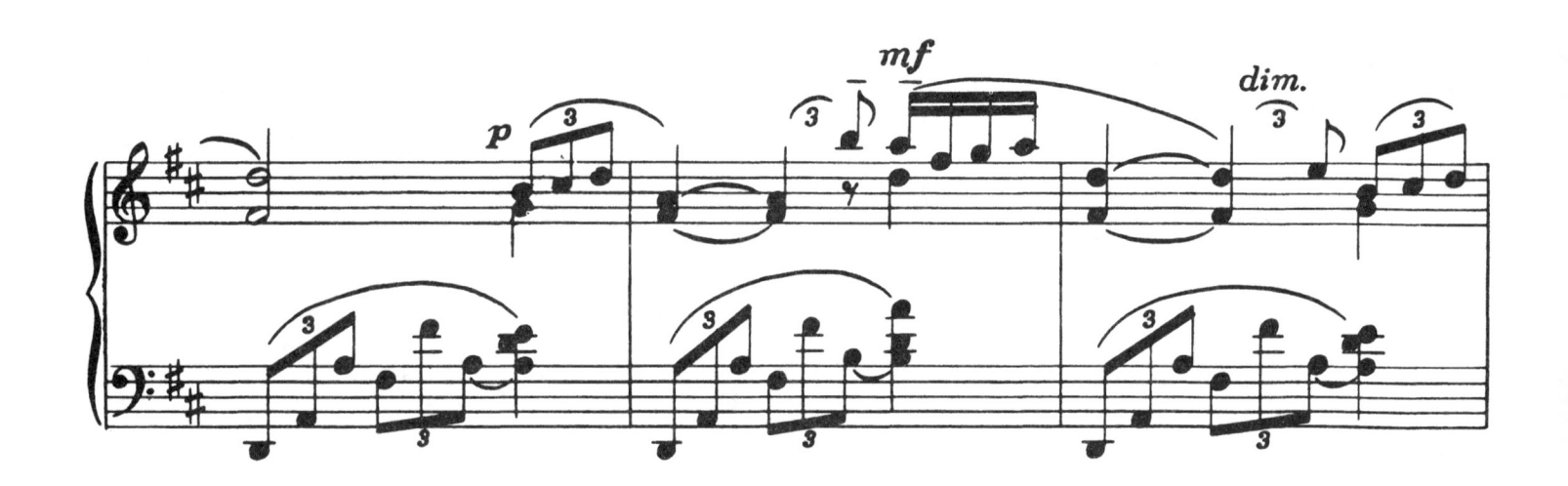

RHAPSODIE ON A THEME OF PAGANINI, OP. 43

By SERGEI RACHMANINOFF

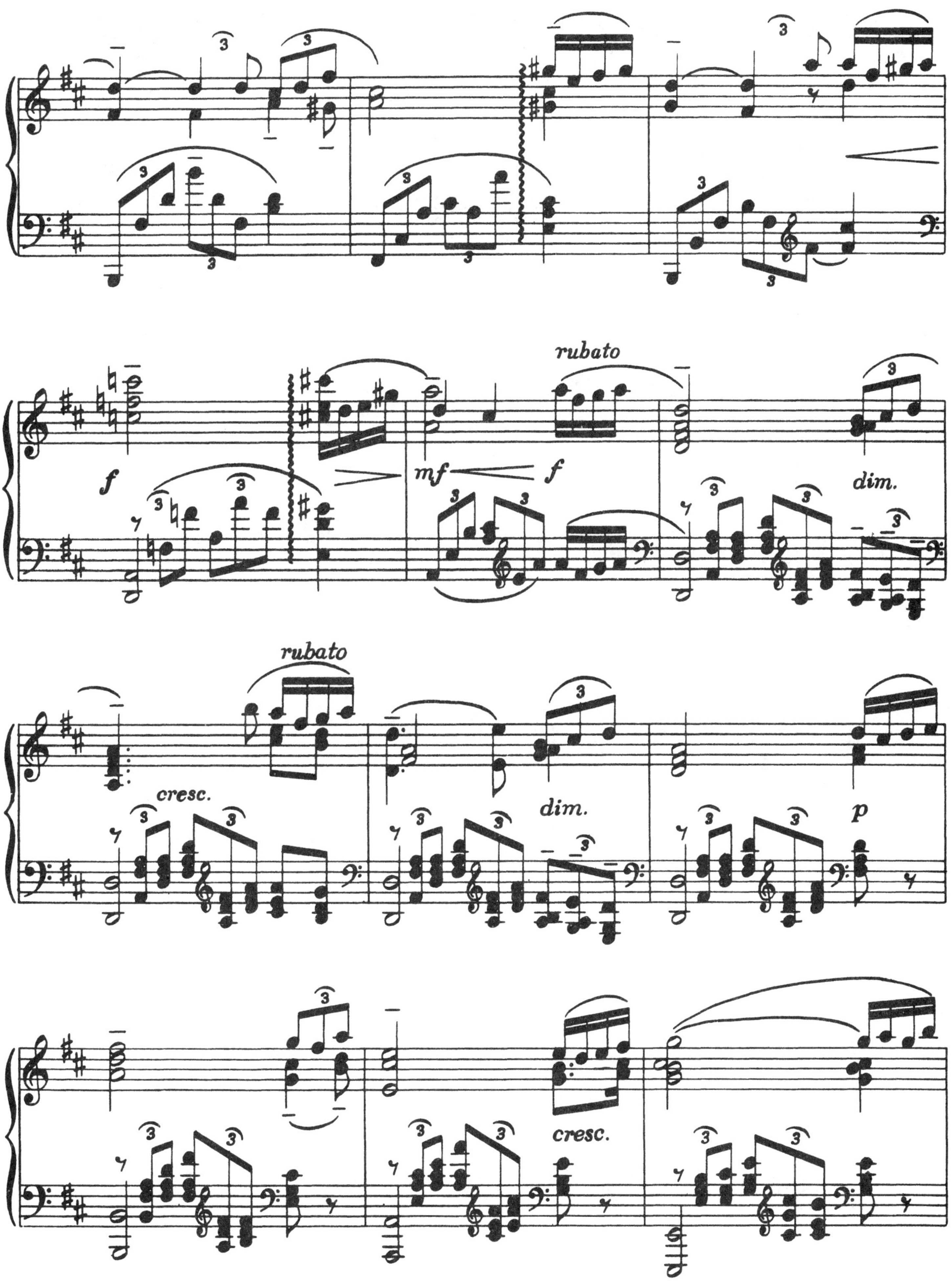
rubato
f
mf
f
dim.
rubato
cresc.
dim.
p
cresc.

Rhapsodie on a Theme of Paganini, Op. 43

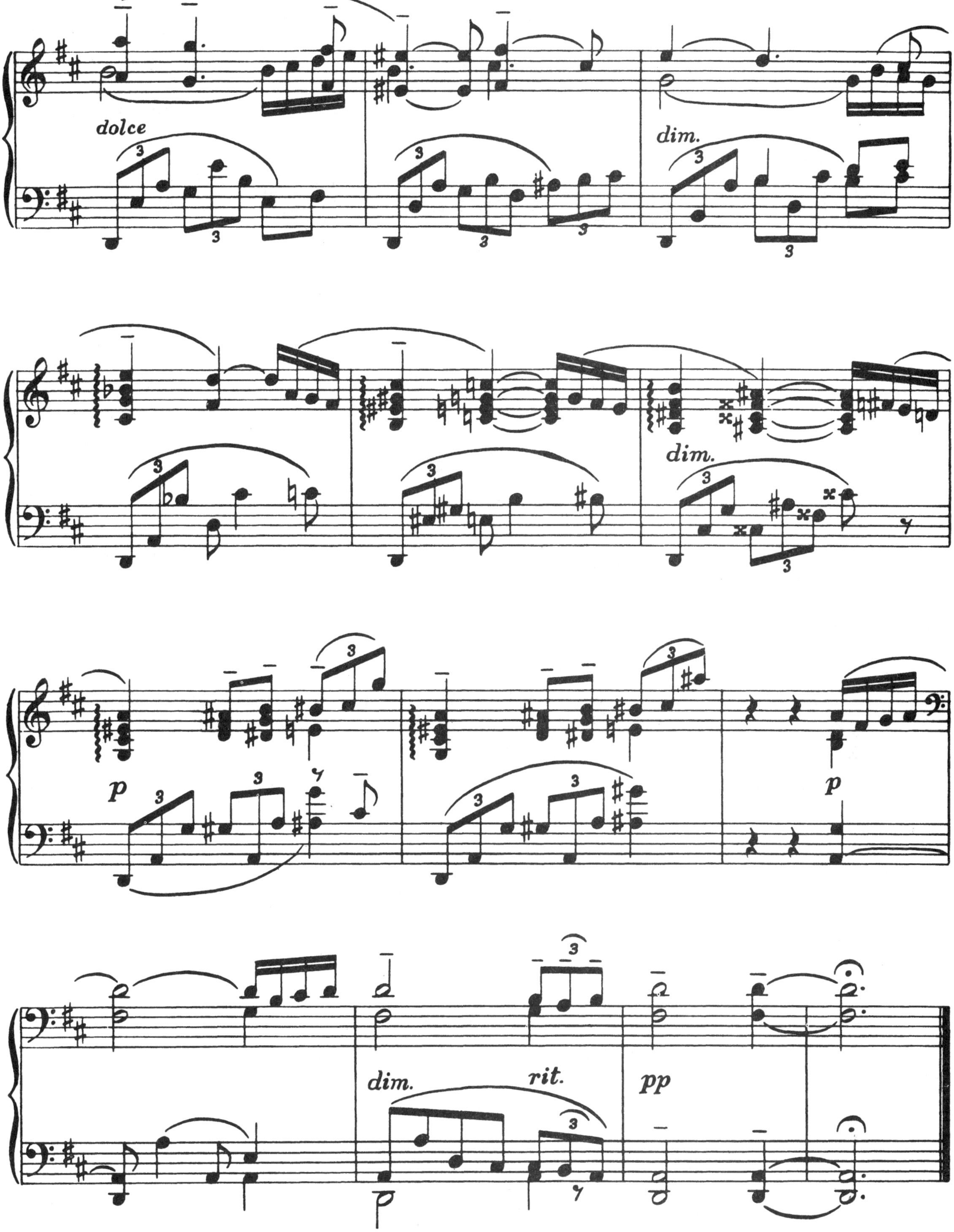
dolce
dim.
dim.
p
p
dim.
rit.
pp

THE MASTERPIECE
(Theme from *"Masterpiece Theater"*)

By J.J. MOURET and PAUL PARNES

The Masterpiece - 3 - 1

© 1972 (Renewed) SEPTEMBER MUSIC CORPORATION
All Rights Reserved

D
A/C♯
D
A/C♯ D
1.
Bm
G
A
2.
2nd time
al Coda
A7
D
ritard 3rd.time
Fine 3rd. time
G
C
A7
B
Em
C
F

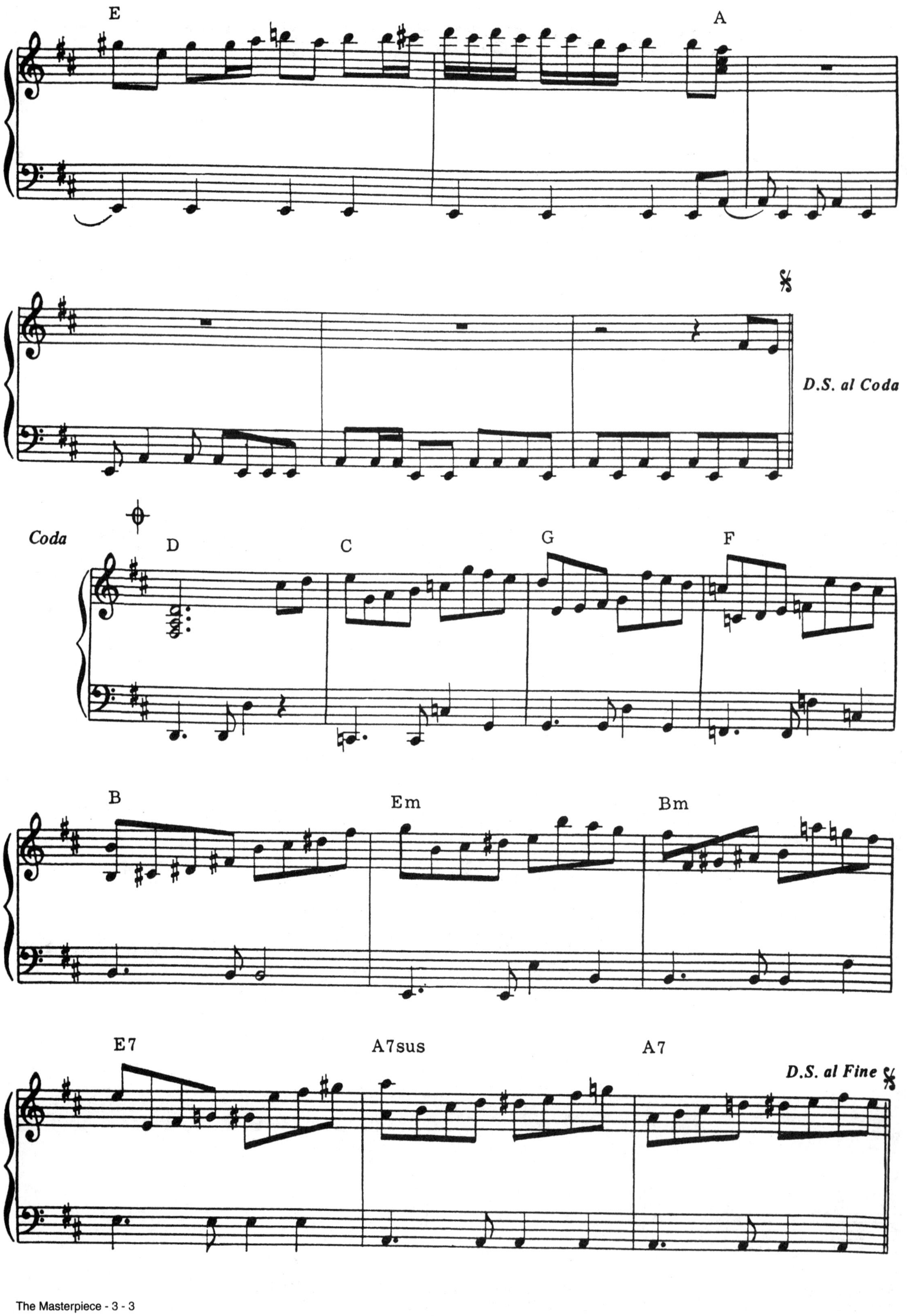
E
A
D.S. al Coda
Coda
D
C
G
F
B
Em
Bm
E7
A7sus
A7
D.S. al Fine

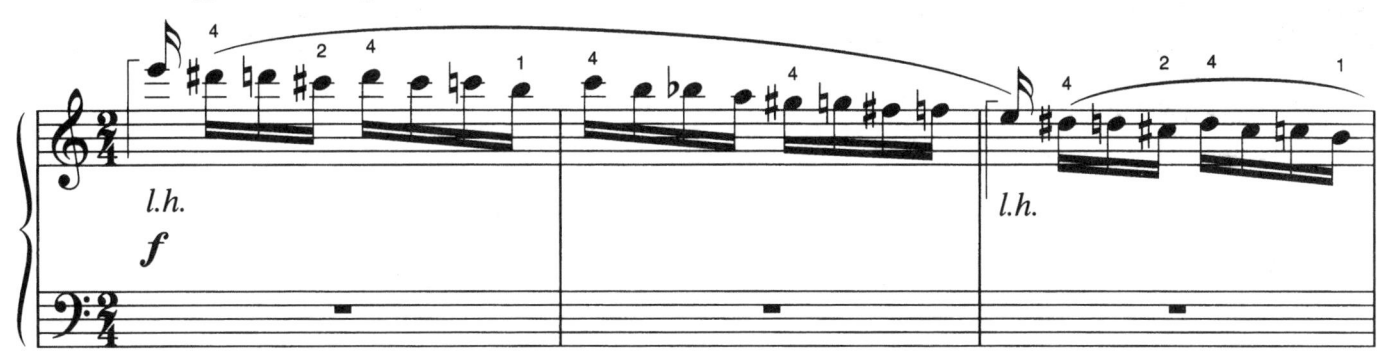

FLIGHT OF THE BUMBLE BEE

By NIKOLAI RIMSKY-KORSAKOV

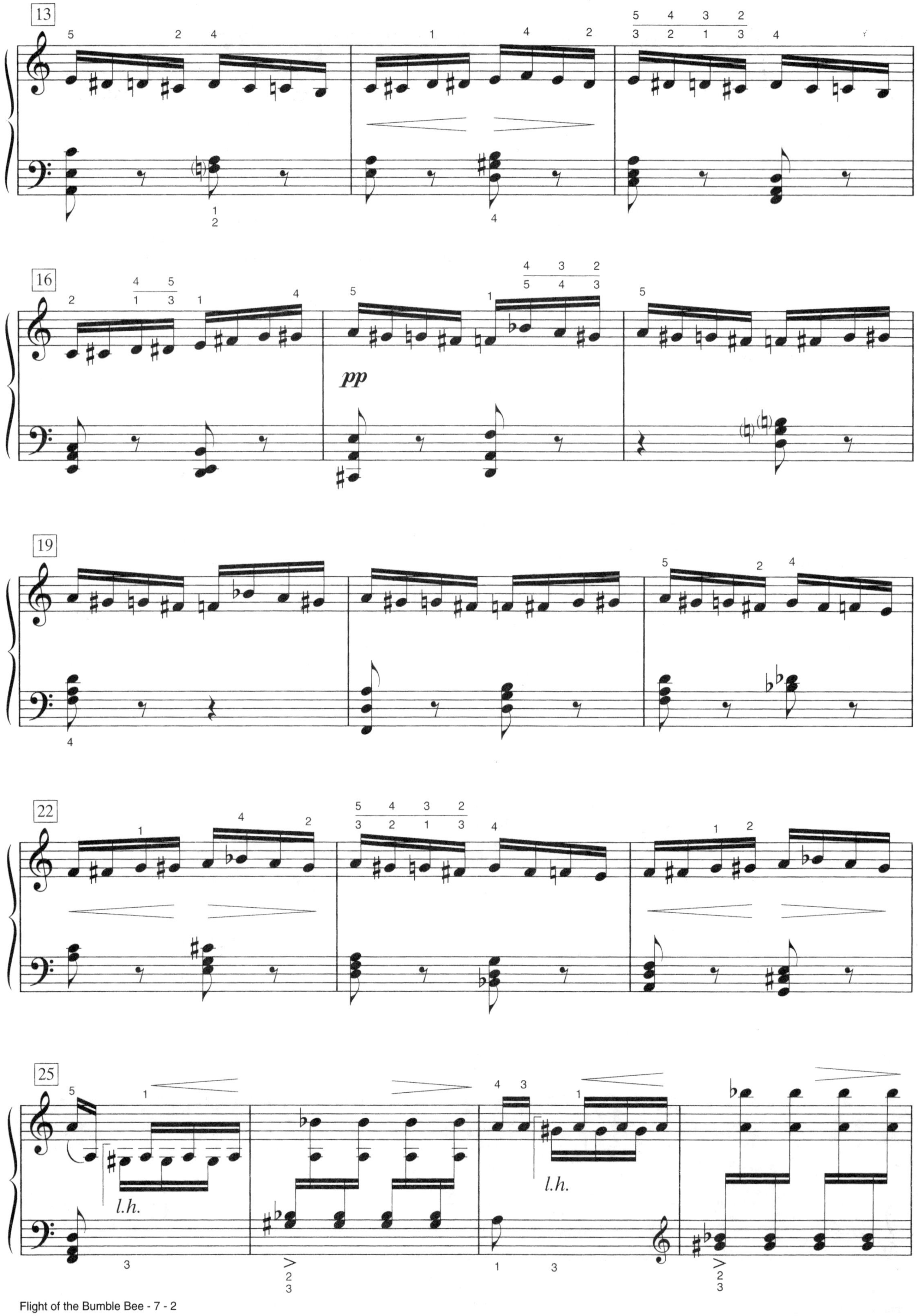
13
16
pp
19
22
25
l.h.
l.h.

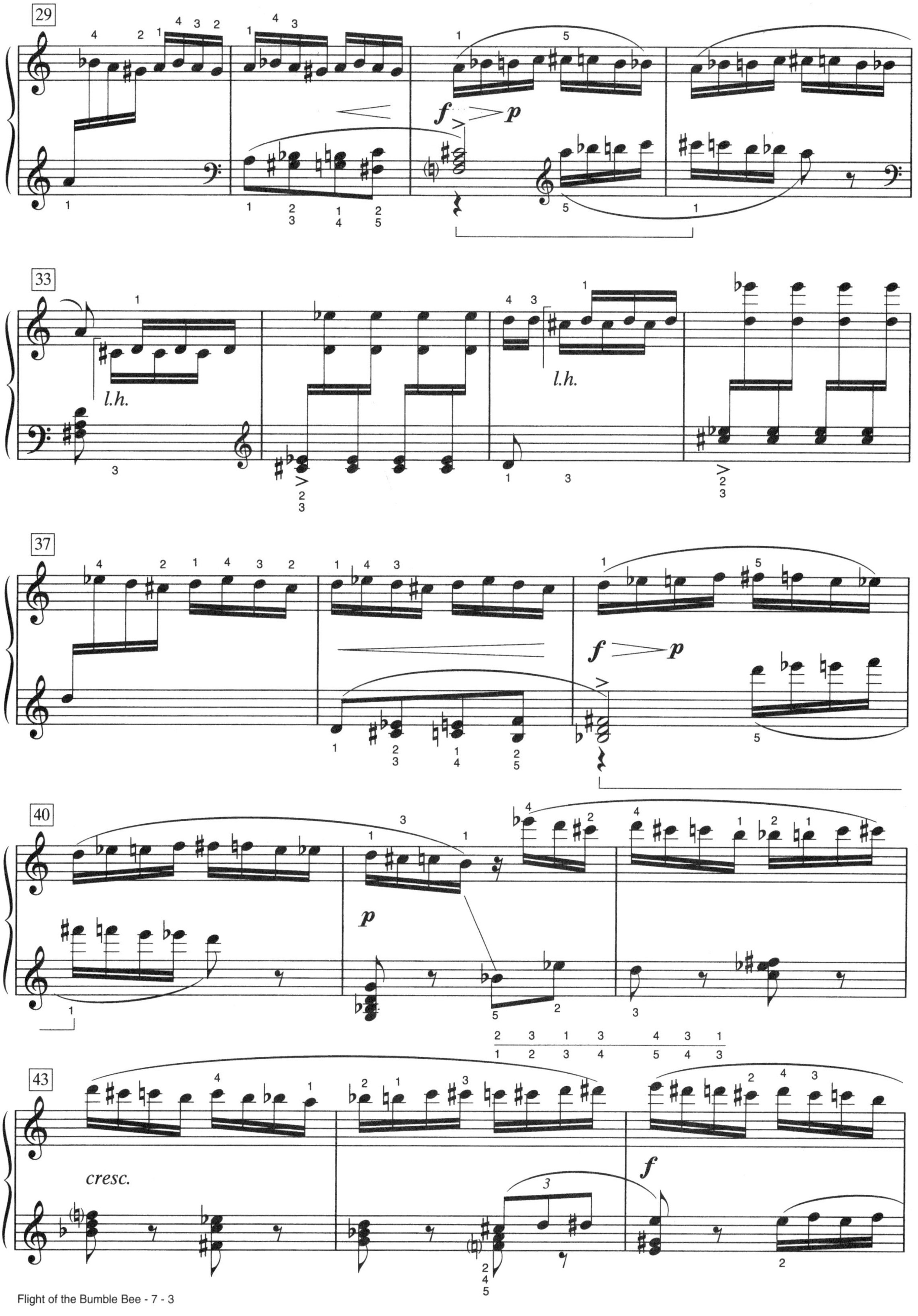
29
33
l.h.
l.h.
37
40
43
cresc.

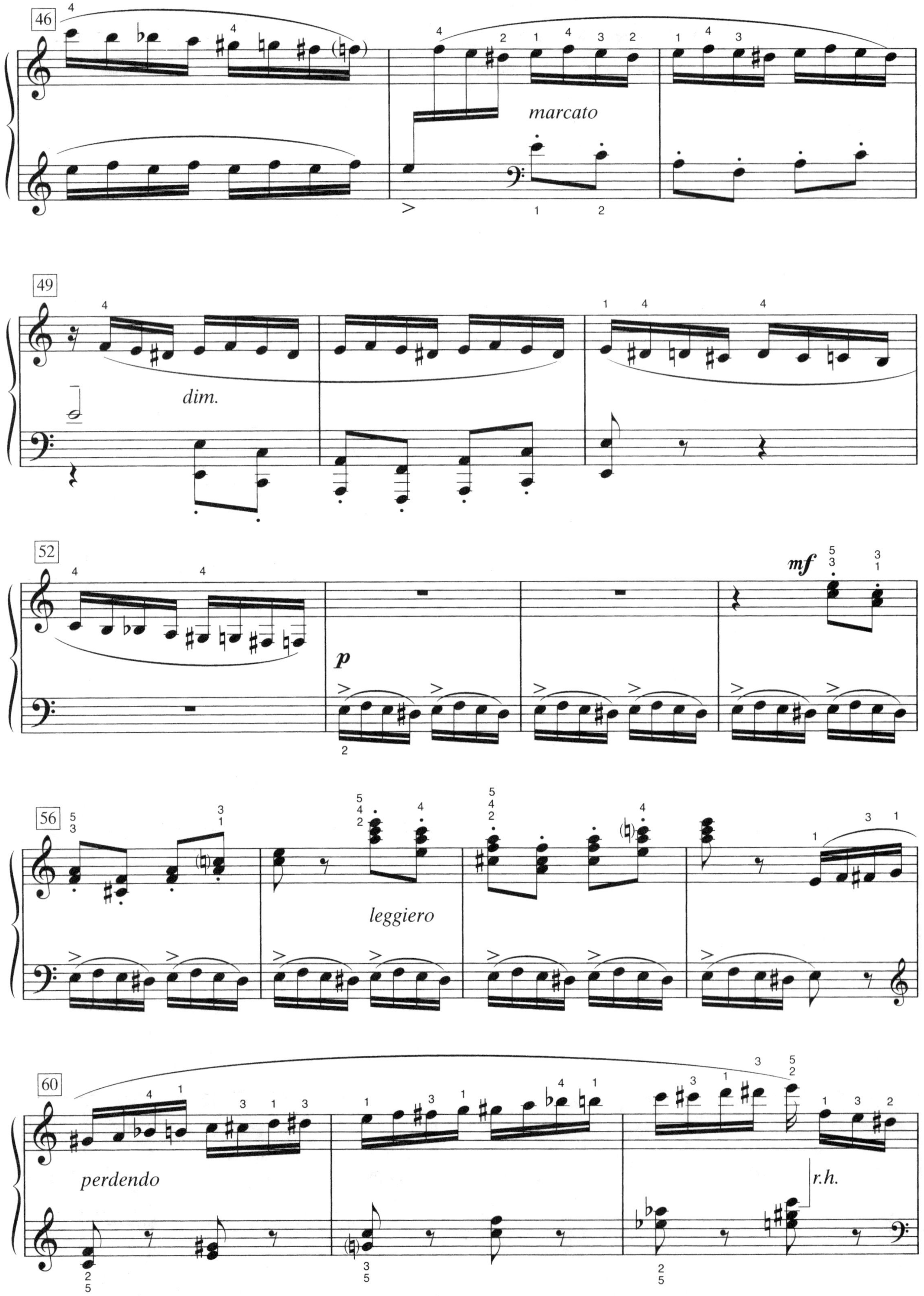
46
marcato
49
dim.
52
mf
p
56
leggiero
60
perdendo
r.h.

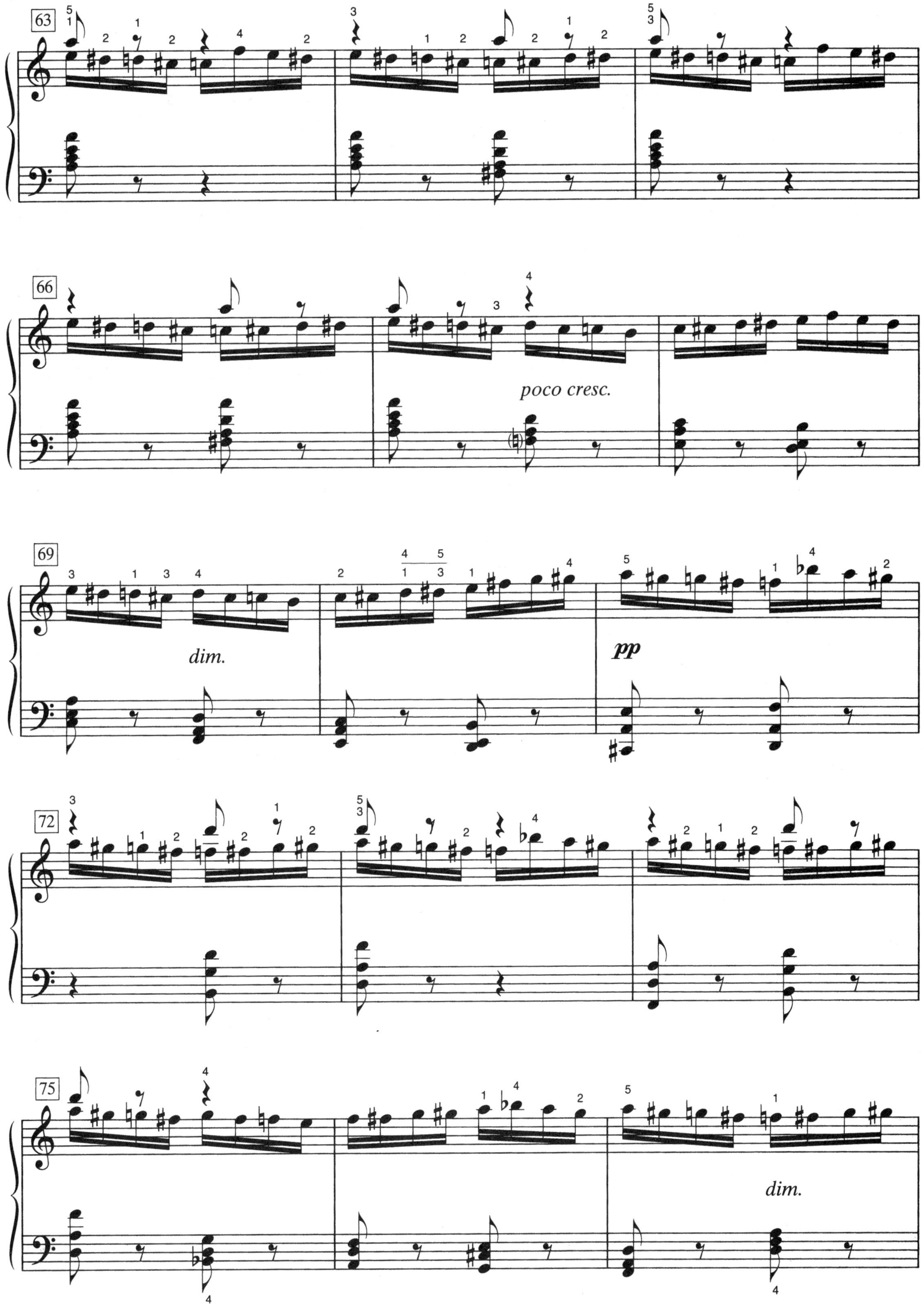
63
66
poco cresc.
69
dim.
pp
72
75
dim.

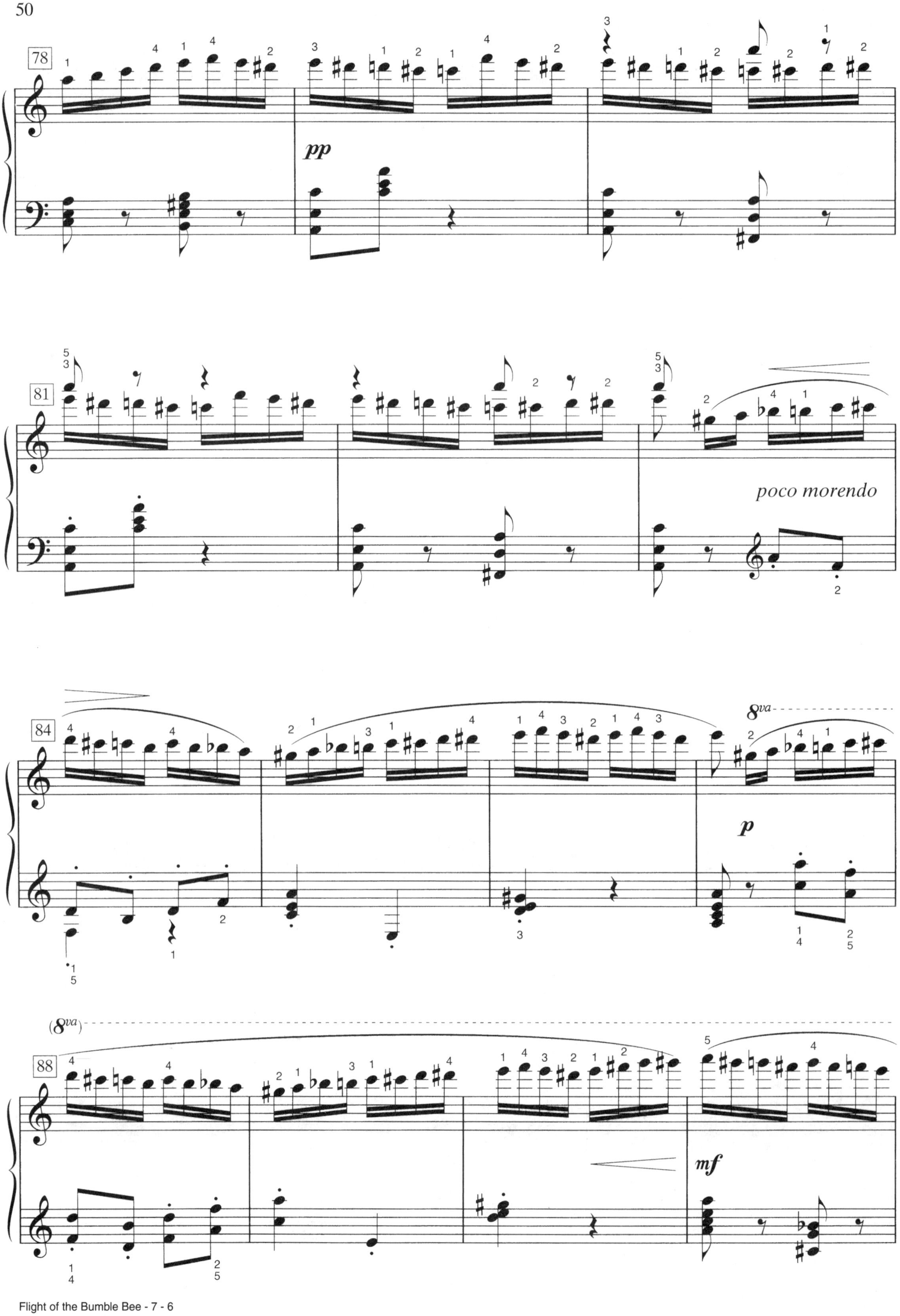
78
pp
81
poco morendo
84
8va
p
88
(8va)
mf

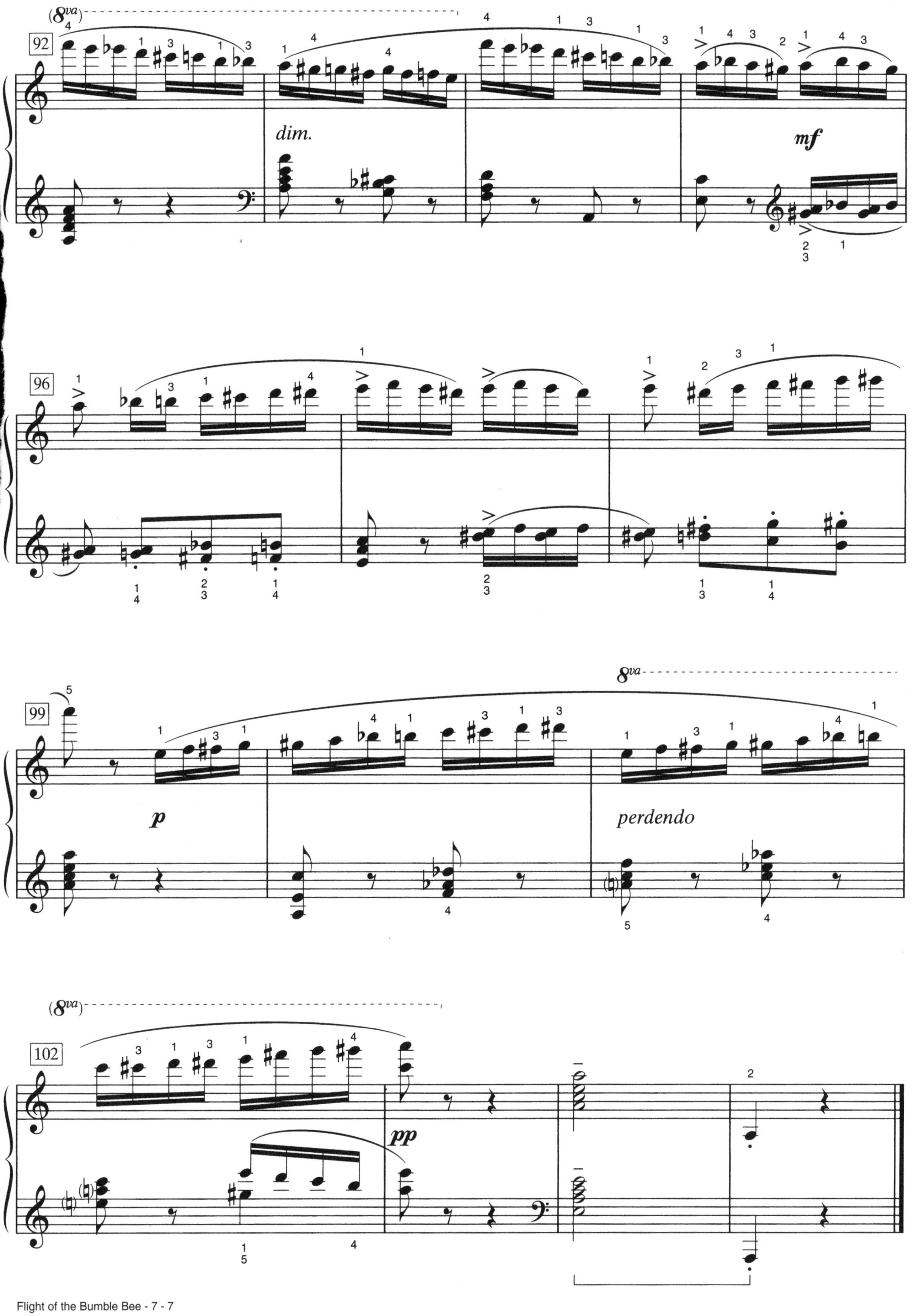
dim.
mf
p
perdendo
pp

Alfred